The Light You Shine Begins With You

Written by Sue Frampton
Illustrated by Rosemary Carroll

Written by Sue Frampton
Illustrated by Rosemary Carroll

Printed Worldwide
First Printing 2026
First Edition 2026

ISBN 979-8-9956377-1-4

Interior Book Design by Walt's Book Design
www.waltsbookdesign.com

For information about permission to reproduce any selections from this book or to communicate with the author, please email: thelightyoushinebeginswithyou@gmail.com

Ages 3 to 8
Keywords: mindfulness, grounding, calming, emotions, nature, kindness, meditation

This book is lovingly dedicated to my three children—Jonathan, Rebekah, and Benjamin—and to my three grandchildren—Alexander, Isabella, and Gabriella.
Each of you is uniquely special in your own beautiful way. May you always be your authentic selves and experience a life filled with peace, joy, and love.

This book belongs to:

The Light You Shine Begins With You

There's magic dancing everywhere,
In wind and sun and swirling hair.
It fills kites that make them rise.
It heats the Earth. It shines in skies.

It makes the rivers run and flow.
It helps the tiniest seedlings grow.
It's in a squirrel and in a tree.
This magic is pure energy!

The sun radiates, warm and bright.
It fills our days with golden light.
It gently touches leaf and tree.
It's sunshine's gift — pure energy!

The waves that crash, the rain that pours,
The lightning flash and thunder roars-
It's all energy at play,
In earth's great dance, both night and day.

The wind fills sails that travel the sea,
A moving breath of energy.
The grass is soft and the earth is warm,
A steady strength in every storm.

The sun, the wind, the earth, the sea–
They share their power endlessly.
And you, dear child, are glowing too,
With that same energy in you.

When feelings rush or thoughts feel bad,
When days feel busy, lonely or sad,
You have a way to calm inside.
The earth is always by your side.

Go outside and hug a tree,
Or lie on the ground so you feel free.
Take three deep breaths very slow.
Breathe in...breathe out...and let them go.

Close your eyes and gently see
A bright light resting quietly.
Imagine it above your head,
A golden glow that softly spreads.

Let it travel down inside,
Through your heart and arms so wide,
Through your belly, legs, and feet—
A soothing light, calm and sweet.

Imagine roots growing from your feet.
Going down with a steady beat.
The calming energy deep in the ground
Is holding you, safe and sound.

Pull the energy up from the earth below.
Feel your steady heartbeat slow.
You are grounded. You are bright.
You are peaceful. You are light.

Now choose one loving thing to do,
Something kind that feels like you.
A smile, a share, a helping hand,
A gentle heart that takes a stand.

Your light shines when you are calm and kind-
A peaceful body, a thoughtful mind.
Grounded, steady, brave and true-
The light you shine begins with you.

~ THE END ~

About the Author

Sue Frampton is a teacher at heart who believes in the quiet magic of the world around us. Inspired by her own journey of growth and discovery, she began writing to help children understand something simple but powerful—that everything is made of energy, including them. Through gentle, imaginative storytelling, Sue hopes to give children tools to feel calm, grounded, and connected to the Earth beneath their feet. Her work is designed not only for little ones, but also for the grown-ups who read alongside them, offering moments of peace, wonder, and connection for all. When she's not writing, Sue enjoys spending time in nature, noticing the small, beautiful details that often become the seeds of her inspiration.

About the Illustrator

Rosemary Carroll is an author, illustrator and publisher specializing in custom children's picture books through her company Fifth Avenue Press. She has created work for New York socialites, physicians, teachers, business professionals, cruise lines, and notable institutions, including The Plaza Hotel in New York City. Her signature illustration of a Cavalier King Charles Spaniel holding the key to the The Plaza was displayed in the hotel's lobby for years, highlighting her distinctive style and storytelling. In her latest collaboration, "The Light You Shine Begins With You" by Sue Frampton, Rosemary brings the story to life through her unique illustrations and publishing expertise. Her joy is inspiring young readers through meaningful and beautifully crafted children's books.

Tips for Parents, Teachers and Caregivers:

Thank you for taking the time to read this book. My intention is for children and adults to live a more positive life. Grounding can help calm the nervous system, reduce stress and improve mood and well-being.

The breathing is most effective when you take a nice deep breath in through your nose. Pretend you are trying to take in a yummy smell or trying to keep your nose from running. Feel your chest rise as your lungs fill with air. You can count in your head; one, two, three as you breath in. Hold it for three seconds and then slowly blow the air out your mouth like you are cooling off your soup or trying to blow out candles on a birthday cake. As you get used to doing this, increase to 4 breaths in, hold for 4, blow out for 4. This is called box breathing and it helps to slow down your breathing to relax you and; when done properly, can reset the fight/flight response.

Grounding does not have to be done outside but may be more effective. You can use your imagination through guided visualization as the book talks you through it. Walking outside in the grass, soil or sand is another way of grounding.

Acknowledgement

I am so grateful for the incredible people who guided and supported me along this journey. Meeting Nicole Lawler opened the doorway to this way of thinking. Mandy Morris helped expand it even further, encouraging me to create something that serves the greater good of the universe. Michael Beckwith became a daily source of inspiration through his podcast, and it was during one of his meditations that the seed for this book was planted—a vision to uplift children and give them tools for a more peaceful life.

I'm especially thankful for Rosemary Carroll who taught a class about writing children's books. Rosemary had such warmth and enthusiasm for everyone's ideas in class. I felt a soul connection the moment I met her. She so generously took me under her wing after the class, sharing her wisdom and guiding me through the book writing process. She agreed to be my illustrator and was great to work with.

I'm also deeply grateful for Dr. Reverend Kathleen Johnson and Candace Berkowitz for nurturing both my body and soul throughout this process and finally, my dear friend, Amy O'Donald—my biggest cheerleader—who supported and lifted me up every step of the way, even when others questioned my path.

Please visit and follow my facebook page
The Light You Shine Begins With You
My website: www.thelightyoushine.com

See updates, events, inspiration, challenges and triumphs.
Stay tuned for more books in my Mind, Body, Spirit & Science series.

If you enjoyed the book, please go to Amazon to review the book.

$12.95
ISBN 979-8-9956377-1-4

www.ingramcontent.com/pod-product-compliance
Lightning Source LLC
LaVergne TN
LVHW070203110826
845147LV00002B/481
9798995637714